YOU CHOOSE

CAN YOU DISCOVER
THE LOST DUTCHMAN'S
GOLD MINE?

AN INTERACTIVE TREASURE ADVENTURE
BY THOMAS KINGSLEY TROUPE

CAPSTONE PRESS
a capstone imprint

Published by Capstone Press, an imprint of Capstone
1710 Roe Crest Drive
North Mankato, Minnesota 56003
capstonepub.com

Library of Congress Cataloging-in-Publication Data
Names: Troupe, Thomas Kingsley, author.
Title: Can you discover the Lost Dutchman's gold mine? : an interactive treasure
  adventure / Thomas Kingsley Troupe.
Description: North Mankato, MN : Capstone Press, [2024] | Series: You choose:
  Treasure hunters | Includes bibliographical references. | Audience: Ages 8 to 12.
  Audience: Grades 4-6.
Summary: Your brother went missing looking for the Lost Dutchman's Gold Mine
  in the Arizona mountains and you have several paths to pursue, some of which
  may get you killed, and it is up to the reader to decide which way you will go.
Identifiers: LCCN 2022050291 (print) | LCCN 2022050292 (ebook) |
  ISBN 9781669032106 (hardcover) | ISBN 9781669032076 (paperback)
  ISBN 9781669032083 (pdf)
Subjects: LCSH: Gold mines and mining—Arizona—Juvenile literature.
  Legends—Arizona—Juvenile literature. | Plot-your-own stories. | LCGFT:
  Choose-your-own stories.
Classification: LCC TN423.A75 T76 2024 (print) | LCC TN423.A75 (ebook)
DDC 622/.342209791—dc23/eng/20230214
LC record available at https://lccn.loc.gov/2022050291
LC ebook record available at https://lccn.loc.gov/2022050292

Editorial Credits
Editor: Aaron Sautter; Designer: Bobbie Nuytten; Media Researcher:
Rebekah Hubstenberger; Production Specialist: Whitney Schaefer

Photo Credits
Alamy: POL/BT, 106 (middle), TMI, 85; Getty Images: KenWiedemann, 42,
Remo Daut/500px, 102; Shutterstock: Abbie Warnock-Matthews, 9, Andrey_
Kuzmin, design element (map), 106–107 (background), Cheri Alguire, 12,
Christopher PB, 79, Flugklick, cover (bottom left), Gilmanshin, 107 (bottom),
IrinaK, 75 (top left), John D Sirlin, 6, josefauer, 1 (pickax), kramynina, 25, Manuela
Durson, 71, Mishainik, cover (background), 1 (background), n_defender, 47, 57,
Net Vector, design element (light), Paul A Smith, 87, Raisa Nastukova, 72, Rusty
Dodson, 75 (top right), Stanley Ford, 95, TinnitusDoll, 28, UMB-O, 32, Vasilev
Evgenii, 62, walter_g, 107 (top right); Superstition Mountain Historical Society:
Greg Davis Collection, 45, 81 (all)

TABLE OF CONTENTS

About Your Adventure

You're worried about your brother. About a month ago, James left for Arizona to try to find the Lost Dutchman's Gold Mine. It's been an obsession of his for years, and he finally made the trek alone.

James promised to call when he got there, but it's been weeks since you've heard from him. You need to find your brother. And, if you're lucky, maybe you'll find the lost mine too!

Chapter One sets the scene. Then you choose which path to read. Follow the directions at the bottom of the page as you read the stories. The decisions you make will change your outcome. After you finish one path, go back and read the others for new perspectives and more adventures.

Turn the page to begin your adventure.

The Superstition Mountains are located in the desert just east of Phoenix, Arizona.

CHAPTER 1

WHERE DID YOU GO, BRO?

You're trying to leave another message for your brother, James. But his voicemail is telling you that his inbox is full. That's never a good sign. You're probably not the only one looking for him.

It's been more than two weeks since you last heard from James. The last time you spoke with him, he said he was off to search for the fabled Lost Dutchman's Gold Mine. Like other treasure hunters before him, he believed an amazing fortune was hidden somewhere around Arizona's Superstition Mountains.

Turn the page.

James didn't tell you exactly where he was going, so you reach out to some of his friends. His friend Marta says that James was going to explore the Superstition Mountains. You almost can't believe that's their real name. After a little research, you learn many treasure hunters have searched for the hidden mine there.

You read countless stories of people who have disappeared near the mountains while hunting for the mine. Other tales tell of discovered skeletons, some headless, in the area. Local farmers overheard the Pima people talk about the strange occurrences, which led to the Superstition Mountains' name.

Some people believe the land is sacred ground to the Apache people. They thought the Thunder God protected the mountains and its treasures. The god was said to strike down anyone who disturbed it.

Visitors to the Superstition Mountains can see several ancient petroglyphs that Indigenous people carved into the rock walls long ago.

But you don't care about old stories and superstitions. You just want to find your brother before something terrible happens. James's friend Marta agrees to go with you, and you book a flight to Phoenix, Arizona.

Turn the page.

As you pack for your flight, you remember James telling you about the mine. He said that many people think the Lost Dutchman's mine is on the eastern side of the mountains. There are no gold deposits on the western range, so the east side seems more likely to have a mine.

While doing research on the plane ride to Arizona, you read about four stones with strange carvings on them. Known as the Peralta Stones, they're on display in a museum near the mountains.

Many believe the stones are a mysterious map that shows the location to the Lost Dutchman's mine. You wonder if studying the stones there first might help you to find the mine and James.

Digging a little deeper into your research, you learn about a German man named Jacob Waltz. In the 1870s, he began paying for things in the area with gold nuggets. No one knew where the gold came from.

Waltz was known as the "Dutchman," even though he wasn't really Dutch. People confused the word "Dutch" with the German word *Deutsch*, which means German.

Waltz claimed he was given the location of the mine by someone from the Peralta family, who originally found the mine.

All signs of the mine and James's location point to the Superstition Mountains area. The problem is, where should you start looking?

To search the eastern side of the mountains, turn to page 13.

To visit Jacob Waltz's final resting place, turn to page 43.

To investigate the Superstition Mountain Museum, turn to page 73.

Several small trails crisscross
the rugged terrain around the
Superstition Mountains.

CHAPTER 2

A MOUNTAIN OF A MISSION

Surely James knew that a lost mine wouldn't be located where no gold could be found. You and Marta decide it would be foolish to look for James and the mine on the western side of the mountains.

You begin your search by looking up some treasure hunter maps online. Many of them point to an area near some taller peaks on the eastern side of the mountains.

James mentioned several times that he wanted to explore the "gaps in the maps." You can only guess that he meant the places where there was no X to mark the spot.

Turn the page.

"Even if we don't find the mine, we should be able to find James," Marta says. "If we shout his name and search enough, he'll turn up."

"Let's hope so," you say with a smile.

When you reach the mountains, you get out of the car and head toward the foothills. The Arizona heat is something you're not sure you'll get used to.

"Wow, it's hot," you say after walking for a few minutes. "Who'd want to spend weeks out here?"

"That would be your brother," Marta says. "But at least it's a dry heat."

Hot is hot, you think, and open your already warm bottle of water. You can't imagine spending a lot of time in the hot desert and mountains, let alone mining in them. Already you miss the air conditioning from the airport.

You walk further and drink plenty of water to stay hydrated. At the base of the mountains, you see what look like trail markers in the sand leading to a cluster of rocks and a small cave. However, the trail goes up the hill and looks like a difficult climb.

Then Marta notices that some brush near a rock face seems to be moving. It could be an animal or the wind. Or maybe it's James!

To climb up and explore the small cave, turn to page 16.

To investigate the moving brush, turn to page 17.

"A cave is a good place to start," you decide, pointing to the entrance. "It could be an old mine."

As you approach the cave, you stop. You sense that something isn't right.

"Why does this place give me the creeps?" Marta whispers. She feels it too, it seems.

"The Pima people were scared of the mountains, too," you remind her. "It's why they're called the Superstition Mountains, after all."

You watch as some small rocks bounce and fall against the rock face. You're almost afraid to go into the cave if the mountain is that unstable. You call out for your brother, but there's no answer.

Marta is backing up. Something about the cave is spooking her.

To back up with Marta, turn to page 19.

To ignore the bad feelings and go into the cave, turn to page 21.

You decide to keep pushing forward.
It's unlikely that the cave near the base of the mountain could be the lost gold mine. You're also sure your brother got further than this in his search.

You and Marta forge ahead and climb up the slope toward the brush. As you get closer, Marta points at the foliage.

"It's weird the way the plants are blowing around a bit," she says. "Don't you think?"

"Yeah," you reply in agreement. "It is pretty strange."

The plant's leaves appear to be blowing away from the rock face. This seems impossible since wind can't pass through rock. As you get closer, you notice something odd about the side of the mountain. From the angle where you're standing, it doesn't look like rock at all.

Turn the page.

Instead, it seems to be an old, dusty piece of fabric. It almost looks like someone attached it to the side of the rock to hide something. As you get closer, you can feel a slight wind blowing through the gaps and tears in the fabric.

You reach out and touch the fabric. It's old and rough. It looks like someone took the time to paint it so it would blend into the side of the mountain. From far away, no one would ever know it wasn't part of the rock face. The fabric is hiding an opening in the rock.

"What do you think is back there?" Marta whispers. She looks nervous about the camouflage fabric. You wonder if someone, maybe even your brother, is hiding back there.

To pause and call for James, turn to page 23.

To pull the fabric away and see what's inside, turn to page 25.

You don't like the way the rocks are falling down the side of the mountain for no real reason. Is this part of the Lost Dutchman's curse? Is the Thunder God warning you and Marta to stay away?

Either way, going into the cave isn't a great idea. You slowly back away from the mountain and into the scrub brush behind you.

But suddenly, you hear an ominous rattle and feel a sharp pain in your leg. You look down to see a large snake has sunk its fangs into you. You thrash and kick the snake into the brush. It slithers through the sand and rocks, and you lose sight of it.

"Oh no!" Marta's shouting. "That was a speckled rattlesnake!"

"Oh, perfect!" you shout. "Am I going to die?"

Turn the page.

Marta shakes her head.

"No," she says. "Not if we get you treated right away."

You both scramble as best you can away from the area. Marta quickly gets out her cell phone to call for paramedics. Unfortunately, there's no signal out here in the desert. The call doesn't go through.

You realize you need to get back to the car right away and try to find help. Your search for James and the mine had only just begun, but for now it looks like it's over.

THE END

To follow another path, turn to page 11.
To learn more about the Lost Dutchman's Gold Mine, turn to page 103.

You're not sure what's happening and frankly, you don't care. You're going into that cave. You're determined to save James, find the lost mine, or both!

As you head toward the cave entrance, you can hear the mountain rumbling, almost as if it's alive. You glance up to see a massive boulder rolling toward you, followed by more large rocks. You try to duck out of the way, but it's too late. You're pinned underneath the giant rock. The pain is overwhelming, and you're pretty sure nearly every bone in your body is broken.

While you gasp in pain, you hear an old man's voice shouting at Marta.

"You got no business in these parts!" he says. "I've been searching for Dutchie's gold for decades. No city folk are gonna steal it from me!"

Turn the page.

"We were just looking for his brother!" Marta cries.

"That don't make no difference to me, lady!" the old prospector growls. "Now git! Or I'll squash you like your dumb friend!"

Were you close to finding the mine? You'll never know for sure. You just know the old guy doesn't take kindly to trespassers.

As you feel yourself fade away, you can hear Marta promise to send help. But you have a feeling that in a few minutes, it's not going to matter.

THE END

To follow another path, turn to page 11.
To learn more about the Lost Dutchman's Gold Mine, turn to page 103.

You hesitate to pull back the fabric. You have no idea what or who might be hiding back there. Instead, you decide to call out for your brother. If James is hiding back there, maybe he'll give you some sort of sign or let you know it's safe.

As soon as you shout his name, you hear dusty footsteps approaching. The fabric is yanked to the side, and four dirty, angry-looking men approach.

One aims a pistol at you. The others carry pickaxes and a shovel. They're not happy to see you. The one holding the shovel grumbles something about "trespassers" and "treasure seekers" and then spits.

The men order you to get on your knees. Without any weapons to fight back, you have no choice. They tie your hands behind your back and lead you and Marta back down the mountain and further into the desert.

Turn the page.

You have a bad feeling about this.

When it feels like you've been walking forever, they stop. The men untie you and Marta, then they make you each dig a hole in the sand. When the holes are deep enough, they order both of you to climb into them. Once inside the holes, the men bury you and Marta in dirt and sand, leaving only your heads exposed. Then the men leave you and Marta to your fate.

Looking around, you see skulls sticking out of the ground nearby. You realize that if you and Marta can't wiggle your way free, you'll be the next skulls in the desert. If you do manage to get free, you're going home. Hunting for your brother and lost treasure in the desert is too dangerous!

THE END

To follow another path, turn to page 11.
To learn more about the Lost Dutchman's Gold Mine, turn to page 103.

You realize you won't find your brother, let alone the mine, if you don't take a chance. After a deep breath, you pull the fabric aside.

To your surprise, you find a square entrance that looks like an old mine shaft. Could this be it? You turn on your flashlight and move carefully into the mine. You see fresh footprints in the dirt.

"Those could be from James," Marta says. "They look like boot prints—and his size, too!"

Turn the page.

"I sure hope so," you whisper.

You notice a few other tracks beside the boot prints. Did James explore the mine with someone else? Maybe they're not his at all. Or worse, maybe he ran into unexpected company.

As you move further into the mine, you see a faint light ahead. There's someone else in here! You take another step and listen carefully. The voices don't sound like your brother or anyone else you know. Could they be other treasure seekers or miners from the area?

Soon you hear footsteps approach. You quickly duck behind some old boxes of ore and click off your flashlight. But you were so focused on the sounds ahead of you that you didn't notice someone approach from behind. You feel strong hands roughly grab your shoulder.

To try to break free and escape, go to page 27.
To call for help, turn to page 29.

You're no fighter, but you don't have a choice. You twist out of the man's grip and throw a punch. Your fist smashes against his jaw, and he staggers back, hitting his head on a wooden support beam.

As he tries to shake it off, Marta picks up a shovel and smacks him on the top of the head. The series of blows knocks him out. He falls, and you quickly drag him behind the boxes.

Then you hear a voice shout from deeper in the tunnel.

"Hey, Curtis! That you?"

Marta nods toward another passage in the mine. It's time to move! The two of you run down the passage and into the deep darkness.

You're too afraid to turn on your flashlight just yet. The others might spot the light. But it's dangerous to move in the dark without it.

Turn the page.

Before long, you hear heavy footsteps behind you. Then you hear someone shout. You're pretty sure they just found Curtis lying behind the boxes. You must escape and hope you don't get lost in the old mine.

To use your flashlight and run, turn to page 31.
To stay hidden in the dark, turn to page 33.

You don't know who's grabbing you, but maybe the others will help you. As you grapple with the brute, you shout out. Marta tries to pull the thug off of you.

Seconds later, you hear the men further in the mine shaft react and run toward you. But before they can get to you, the man has you pinned to the ground. One of the other men stops Marta from hitting your opponent.

"Who'd you find, Curtis?" a man with a patchy beard says. There are gold teeth in his mouth, and his breath stinks. Calling out resulted in you and Marta getting captured.

They take you both to another part of the mine where it looks like they've been digging. You don't see any gold, so you wonder if this was the Lost Dutchman's mine or not.

Turn the page.

They tie the two of you to a wooden post that supports the rock ceiling above you. One of them mutters something about finding the other one, and you wonder who he's talking about.

Another man asks where his machete is. You look down and see a machete at your feet. Are they planning to use the big blade on you? You won't be able to pick it up, but you can kick it away. That might draw their attention, though.

To wait for another way out, turn to page 35.

To kick the machete away, turn to page 37.

"We need to turn on our lights," you whisper.

"Won't they see us?" Marta replies.

"Let's hope not," you say and turn on your flashlight.

Marta does the same, and you both run past a huge crevasse in the mine. It's a good thing you had your lights on. You could have fallen into the deep hole otherwise.

"That was close," you whisper. Marta nods her head and smiles.

You quickly duck down a shaft, squeeze through a tight tunnel, and find yourself next to an old mine cart with a lantern on the front. The rusty cart sits on old tracks that lead deeper into the mountain. There's another set of tracks next to it, but there's no cart.

Turn the page.

Mine carts were pushed on tracks to transport ore or minerals from deep inside a mine.

You hear voices in the distance. It's unclear if they know where you and Marta have gone. You could try to sneak by the men without getting caught. But maybe you can make your escape in the mine cart.

To take the mine cart, turn to page 39.

To try to slip past the men, turn to page 41.

There's no way you're turning on your flashlight. You might as well send a beacon to let the bad guys know exactly where you are.

"Let's keep it dark," you whisper.

"You think that's a good idea?" Marta says. "Who knows what we'll run into?"

"Hopefully it won't be any of those creeps looking for us," you reply.

You and Marta quickly slink away from your hiding space as footsteps approach.

"I think they're over here!" you hear one man shout. "Where are all these unwanted visitors coming from? Did that tarp come loose again?"

Unwanted visitors? You wonder what that means. *Was he talking about James?*

You don't get a chance to think about it, because you suddenly step into nothingness!

Turn the page.

You feel yourself falling into an even deeper darkness. Marta shrieks as she falls into the pit too. You bounce off the side of rock walls on your way down. You land on a series of stalagmites that break just about every bone in your body.

With your remaining strength, you turn on your flashlight to find a handful of old skeletons. They apparently had the same "not so bright" idea. Now you and Marta will be joining them in the dark, forever.

THE END

To follow another path, turn to page 11.
To learn more about the Lost Dutchman's Gold Mine, turn to page 103.

Kicking the machete away will only draw attention to you and the weapon. You think there must be another way out of this mess. You watch as the treasure hunters pack up their gear and look around to see if they've missed anything. One of them picks up the machete and smiles wickedly at you.

"Please untie us," you beg. "We just want to find my brother and go home."

"Is that who that other guy was?" he grumbles and smiles. There aren't many teeth in his mouth.

"Well, his treasure hunting days are over," another man laughs. "And so are yours!"

You can only imagine that they must be talking about James. None of them seem interested in letting you go. They're convinced you're only there to steal their gold.

Turn the page.

As they leave, one of them takes two giant hacks at one of the support posts. The wood begins to splinter and crack, and the rock ceiling above you begins to crumble. They bid you goodbye and dart down the passageway. You struggle with your ropes as the support beam snaps. In moments, tons of rock and dirt bury you and Marta alive.

THE END

To follow another path, turn to page 11.
To learn more about the Lost Dutchman's Gold Mine, turn to page 103.

You decide there's no way you're going to let these guys use a weapon on you. When their backs are turned, you stretch your foot forward and kick the machete with the tip of your shoe. The blade slides across the rock floor and clatters down another dark passage. The treasure hunters perk up when they hear the noise.

"Go check it out," the leader of the group orders. He points to the passage.

One of the others runs toward the sound and disappears into the darkness. But then you hear the sounds of a struggle. A moment later you see your brother, holding the machete to the thug's neck.

"James!" you shout.

You can hardly believe it! You found your brother!

Turn the page.

He orders the others to back off as he holds their partner hostage. After releasing you and Marta, the three of you tie up the treasure hunters. Then you lead them out of the mine and bring them to the authorities. Although the dangerous men are removed and your brother is safe, you decide that treasure hunting is too dangerous. Your adventuring days are over!

THE END

To follow another path, turn to page 11.
To learn more about the Lost Dutchman's Gold Mine, turn to page 103.

It seems risky but going deeper in the mine seems like your best option. You just want to avoid the dangerous men and keep from being captured.

You and Marta push the old cart along the tracks to get it moving toward the hill. As it picks up speed, you jump in and help Marta get in.

You fumble with the lantern and manage to get it lit. It casts a faint light ahead of the cart. You duck through low passages and lean as the cart navigates around twists and turns. Ahead you can see a barrier with timbers strapped across the tracks.

"We're going to crash!" you shout.

"Oh no we're not!" Marta shouts.

She pulls on the brakes, and sparks erupt from the metal wheels. In moments, the cart grinds to a stop.

Turn the page.

You stumble out of the cart and switch on your flashlight.

"Who's out there?" a familiar voice calls out. It's your brother, James! You run forward and find him digging through some rocks.

You all work together to reveal a hidden mine shaft. As you step into the dark room, your flashlight reveals an amazing sight. Gold! Gold nuggets are everywhere. The walls seem to be soaked with the precious ore.

"We found it!" James cries. "The Lost Dutchman's Gold Mine!"

"And we found you," you reply.

It's the find of a lifetime, but you're just happy that you finally found your brother.

THE END

To follow another path, turn to page 11.
To learn more about the Lost Dutchman's Gold Mine, turn to page 103.

"We're in *way* over our heads," Marta whispers.

"I think you're right," you whisper back. You didn't think looking for your brother or the lost mine would be so dangerous.

As the men search for you down another passage, you and Marta quietly sneak past them. Eventually you see the light at the end of the tunnel and head out into the bright Arizona sun.

You're a little disappointed. You didn't find your brother or the lost mine. You decide to call the local authorities and report that James is missing. They'd be better able to deal with the thugs in the mine. It's better to be safe than sorry, right?

THE END

To follow another path, turn to page 11.
To learn more about the Lost Dutchman's Gold Mine, turn to page 103.

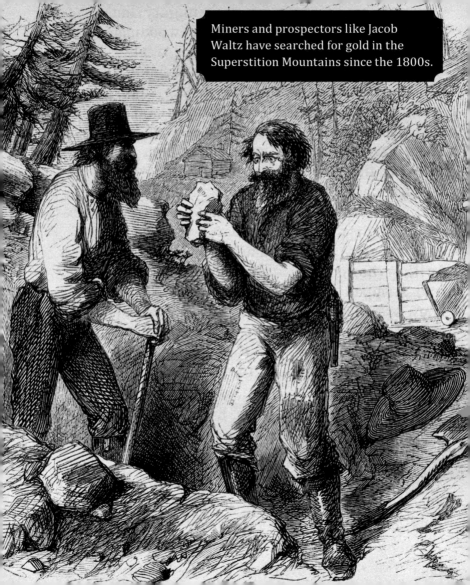

Miners and prospectors like Jacob Waltz have searched for gold in the Superstition Mountains since the 1800s.

CHAPTER 3

A GRAVE DISCOVERY

"Let's start where Waltz ended," you say after getting off the plane at the airport.

"Ah," Marta says. "Clever. We can work our way backward through his life. I like it."

You're not sure why, but visiting the grave of Jacob Waltz, also known as the Lost Dutchman, seems like a good place to start.

You and Marta head toward City Cemetery in search of Waltz's final resting place. You can't help but wonder if there's even a mine to find. It's possible that the people searching for the gold are looking for something that might not exist anymore. That might explain why the Lost Dutchman's mine has never been found.

Turn the page.

You arrive at the cemetery and find Waltz's grave. It's nothing special, just an old grave plot edged with old, rectangular stones. The headstone reads "THE LOST DUTCHMAN" JACOB WALTZ. The years 1808–1891 are carved into it as well.

"Wow," Marta says, squatting closer to the grave. "For someone so infamous, his grave is pretty simple."

"Yeah. You'd think if he was so rich from all that gold, he'd have a nicer headstone," you reply. "Maybe in the end he didn't really care much about all that."

From the research you did on the plane, you know Waltz spent his dying days in bed. He was taken care of by his neighbor, a woman named Julia Thomas. Many believed that she was the only person he told about the hidden mine's location.

Jacob Waltz's grave in Phoenix, Arizona

"Maybe we should see what we can find out about Julia Thomas," you suggest.

Marta shrugs. "That's not a bad idea," she says. "She was probably the last person our friend Mr. Waltz talked to. There might be more information about what she did after he died."

To look for information about Julia Thomas, turn to page 46.

To investigate the grave site further, turn to page 48.

If Waltz trusted Julia Thomas with the location of the mine, maybe she left behind some sort of clue. Could James have thought the same thing? It's worth a shot.

You and Marta head to the nearest library to search for information on Julia Thomas. While digging around, you discover that Julia once led an expedition into the mountains to search for the lost gold. She was joined by a few German miners known as the Petrasch brothers. They spent three weeks in the wilderness trying to find the hidden mine. In the end, they came back only thirsty and empty-handed.

Or did they? Later, Julia began selling maps to the Lost Dutchman's mine and told the story of her adventures to a newspaper. But you're unable to learn if she actually discovered the mine or not.

"Why would Julia sell maps to a mine that she might have never found?" Marta asks.

"Maybe she did find it, but didn't tell the whole story," you reply. "I sure wouldn't let anyone know the location of a whole pile of gold."

You feel like there might be more to Julia's story. Did she lie to the newspaper about the mine? Or were her maps the real deal?

To look for one of Julia Thomas's maps, turn to page 50.

To dig deeper into the newspaper story, turn to page 52.

"I feel like there's something here," you say thoughtfully.

"Like what?" Marta asks. "It's just a dusty old grave."

You're not sure what it is, but something about the grave seems off. You crouch down near the blocks around Waltz's final resting place. One of the stones looks different somehow.

You lean in closer and notice a small *X* carved into the surface of the rock. You brush aside some of the dirt and grit and can see what looks like small, rusty hinges along the side of the rock.

"I'm not sure we should disturb his final—" Marta begins.

But before she can stop you, you carefully pick the fake rock up off the ground and open it. Inside you find a small, rolled-up piece of parchment paper.

Excitedly, you remove the paper and unroll it. Drawn on the paper is a rough map.

"Wow," you say with a big smile on your face. "Waltz literally took the location of the mine to his grave!"

Marta thinks you should bring it to the Superstition Mountain Museum and let them know what you found. But you kind of want to see where the map leads first.

To take the map to the museum, turn to page 54.

To follow the map, turn to page 56.

"Do you think it's possible that any of Julia's maps still exist?" you ask.

"If she made a bunch for would-be treasure hunters, there's got to be at least a photo of one somewhere," Marta replies.

Marta makes a good point. You're suddenly excited by the idea of following a map to find the lost gold. You both take out your phones and begin searching online for a possible lead.

Your research tells you that the map Julia created was based on directions Jacob Waltz gave her as he was dying. Then, after Julia couldn't find the mine herself, she created more copies of the map and sold them.

"Guess they didn't have photocopy machines back then," you mutter.

A moment later, Marta tells you she's found a photo of the map online.

You head to a nearby copy shop to make a print of the map and study it. You start to wonder if Julia truly meant to reveal the location of the mine. What if it was just a fake designed to make money off foolish treasure hunters?

Then you get a wild idea. Instead of following the map that hundreds of others have tried, you could try something different. Instead of going left, you could go right. East could become west. Maybe Julia was trying to hide the mine's true location.

"Might be worth a shot," Marta says with a shrug.

To follow the map as is, turn to page 59.

To follow a map using the opposite directions, turn to page 61.

You decide to find out more about Julia Thomas's connection to the newspaper. You're able to recover fragments of the old story in the newspaper. It talks about how Julia's expedition into the Superstition Mountains was a failure. She made some money selling old maps, but was never known as someone who was wealthy. Marta wonders if Julia was telling the truth.

"What if Julia really did find the gold but didn't want anyone to know?" she asks.

"You think Julia found the lost mine but never bothered to tell anyone?" you reply.

You're not quite sure what to think. As you consider your next move, you get a text message.

"Hey!" you shout. "You're not going to believe this, Marta." You show her your phone.

She's as shocked as you are to see the message from your brother:

SORRY FOR NOT REACHING OUT SOONER. TERRIBLE SERVICE IN THE MOUNTAINS. I'M BACK HOME NOW.

"Well, that's one mystery solved," you say with a shrug.

You call James and learn that he didn't find the mine, but he's safe and sound at home. Not knowing where else to look, you and Marta head to the airport. Guess you'll leave this mysterious treasure hunt to someone else!

THE END

To follow another path, turn to page 11.
To learn more about the Lost Dutchman's Gold Mine, turn to page 103.

"This belongs in a museum," you say, holding up the map. You're sure you heard a famous adventurer say those same words in a movie once.

Marta is right. The map you're holding is an artifact in itself.

The two of you set off for the Superstition Mountain Museum. When you get there, you see a man outside who looks old enough to be one of the museum's exhibits. You explain what you found, and he's more than happy to take the map from you.

As you hand it over, you wonder if you're really doing the right thing. The man is smiling from ear to ear. You don't remember ever seeing someone at a museum look that happy.

"You'll take good care of that, won't you?" Marta says.

"Oh, I will," the man says. He's staring at the map like he's in a trance. "I sure will."

But instead of taking the map inside, the man hops in his car and drives away.

"Why do I get the feeling that guy doesn't actually work for the museum?" you ask.

Marta shakes her head and shrugs. The two of you get into your car to follow him. But you soon discover that he's disappeared.

Congratulations. You just gave your map to a stranger. You're suddenly wishing you'd at least taken a photo of it. Some treasure hunter you are!

THE END

To follow another path, turn to page 11.
To learn more about the Lost Dutchman's Gold Mine, turn to page 103.

"We got lucky and found this map for a reason," you tell Marta. "I think we should use it!"

Marta nods. "Maybe it'll lead us to the Lost Dutchman's mine and hopefully James, too."

You both agree that whether you find the mine or not, you'll give the map to the museum afterward. It's a pretty valuable historical treasure in itself, after all.

The map is easy to follow. Drawings show a narrow gap between some rocks, some sand dunes, and a cluster of boulders. You're able to find all these landmarks without much trouble.

Eventually, you find yourself far out in the desert. As the hot sun shines on you, the map is becoming more difficult to read. Some of the writing is very small.

To use a magnifying glass to read the smaller print, go to page 57.

To squint and read the next part, turn to page 63.

"It's getting really hard to read this thing," you complain.

You reach into your pack and fish out your trusty magnifying glass. It looks like something a detective from an old mystery novel might use.

Although it's your first time on a treasure hunt, you know being precise when following a map is important. You and Marta could easily get lost if you take a wrong turn or end up digging in the wrong spot.

Turn the page.

You position the magnifying glass over the old paper and use it to study the map. It helps you make out details you couldn't see before.

You angle the paper to get the best light to study the map. But as you focus on finding the next marker, you don't notice a wisp of smoke rising from the old paper. Suddenly, the dry old map bursts into flames! You panic and drop the ancient paper. You can only watch as it burns to ashes before your eyes.

"No!" you shout.

You can't believe you burned the map! Treasure hunting obviously isn't for you. Both you and Marta decide to give up looking for the mine and call the local authorities to help find your brother.

THE END

To follow another path, turn to page 11.
To learn more about the Lost Dutchman's Gold Mine, turn to page 103.

"Maybe those other treasure hunters missed something on the map," you say. "We should follow it and see where it leads."

Marta doesn't look convinced. "You think every one of those other fortune seekers read it wrong?"

You shrug. "Anything is possible," you reply.

The map shows the mountains. But there's also a line that leads to somewhere in the desert. You're not sure if the line shows where Julia and her crew went, or potential locations for the mine.

Others have tried and failed to find the gold in the mountains. So, you and Marta decide to try the desert first. You venture out and look for landmarks that match up with Julia's map.

A circle on the map could be a boulder that marks the place to start. You find a boulder nearby that seems to match up with the map.

Turn the page.

You spend the next several hours walking in the blistering hot sun. Finally in the distance you see something gold and shiny along the surface of the sand. Tired, thirsty, and exhausted, you run to the shimmery spot. But as you get closer, the mirage disappears.

When you turn around, Marta is missing. Not even her footprints are there. You can't see the mountains anymore. You're completely lost. Your cell phone is low on battery and overheated. It seems you're in serious trouble. Your brother is missing, and now you will be too.

THE END

To follow another path, turn to page 11.
To learn more about the Lost Dutchman's Gold Mine, turn to page 103.

The map itself might hide some clues. As you study it, you see it leads to several spots in the Superstition Mountains. There are two Xs on the map. You fold it in half to line the Xs up together, then hold it up to the light. You see that the map of the desert has changed.

"Are you making a paper airplane?" Marta asks. "What's with all the folding?"

You show her the "updated" map and she smiles. The two of you go out to the desert and discover that the map now lines up with several rock formations. Now you can follow the clues to where the combined X is.

When you get to the right spot, you pull out your small shovel and start to dig. Almost instantly, you strike something solid. You pull up a small, old box from the ground. You open it and discover a handful of gold nuggets inside. The initials J.W. are carved inside the lid!

Turn the page.

"That's him . . . Jacob Waltz," Marta whispers. She touches the letters gently.

You may not have found the lost mine, but you found one of Jacob Waltz's small gold stashes! Now if only you had a map to find your brother . . . .

THE END

To follow another path, turn to page 11.
To learn more about the Lost Dutchman's Gold Mine, turn to page 103.

You've seen TV shows where a magnifying glass can focus sunlight to start a fire. You realize that holding one over the dry old map isn't a good idea. You definitely don't want to burn up the map!

You squint at the map and see what looks like a boulder with a pointed end. You head into the desert to look for it. After what seems like hours, you spot a rock that looks like the one on the map. You can't be sure it's the right one though.

"Say," Marta says, "where are the mountains?"

You turn and discover that the mountains seem to have disappeared. Could you have traveled that far? You're hot and take a sip of your water. There's not much left, but you're still really thirsty. You check the map. You're still a good distance away from the end of the line.

To drink the rest of your water, turn to page 64.

To save what's left and keep following the map, turn to page 66.

You're just too thirsty. You and Marta decide to share and drink the last of your water. As soon as you're done, you both regret it. There's nothing left for the rest of the journey or the way back—assuming you can find your way back.

You actually feel a little better, but realize you'll need to find more water or you'll be in real trouble. You continue to follow the map, matching up landmarks and getting closer all the time.

After another hour, you begin to feel dizzy and light-headed. You decide it might be best to take a rest right there on the sand and dirt. You close your eyes and fall asleep.

You wake up to the feeling of cold water splashing your face. Above you is a familiar face. It looks like your brother James. Could you be dreaming?

You blink and look again. It's definitely your brother. He helps you up and gives you some more water from his canteen. Instead of you saving him, he's saved you and Marta!

James helps you to his Jeep that's parked in the distance. You reach into your pocket to show him your map, but discover it's long gone. You didn't find the Lost Dutchman's mine. But luckily your brother found you!

THE END

To follow another path, turn to page 11.
To learn more about the Lost Dutchman's Gold Mine,
turn to page 103.

You decide to save your water and conserve it as best you can. You and Marta keep going and wander to the end of the map. You notice for the first time that instead of an *X* at the end of the line, there's a *V*. You look up and wonder if the *V* stands for vultures, since three of them are flying above you in the sky.

That doesn't feel like a good sign.

Marta tells you that some Indigenous people from the area believed vultures were a symbol of bad luck or danger.

Looking down, you notice something strange in the sand. There appears to be a stone, but the way it's shaped looks a little too perfect, too . . . square. You brush the sand away and discover what looks like a step. You dig a little more, only to find another step.

"We need to find water," Marta says. "Not dust the desert."

"I think I found something," you say through your parched throat.

"I'm so thirsty," Marta wheezes.

You're thirsty too and know the work will make you even more so. You glance over and see a cactus nearby. You remember reading something about getting water from a cactus.

To keep digging and hope for the best, turn to page 68.

To cut the cactus open for water, turn to page 70.

"We'll find water in a minute," you insist.

You decide to ignore your thirst. You pull out a small shovel from your pack and keep digging. It's hot and sweaty work, but before long, you and Marta uncover seven steps leading down into the ground. At the bottom of the steps is a small door.

You push on the door and the old, brittle wood snaps, revealing an opening.

"You broke the door," Marta says, wiping the sweat from her forehead.

"I don't think anyone will notice," you reply as you push away some of the splintered wood.

When you climb through the opening and turn on your flashlight, you see gold. Lots and lots of mined gold!

"Are you kidding me?" Marta cries. She suddenly doesn't seem so thirsty anymore.

"I think we actually found something!" you cry, dropping the shovel on the stone floor.

You've found Jacob Waltz's lost vault! Or at least one of them.

It's just then that you realize the *V* on the map stands for vault, not vultures! You can't believe your luck. You can only hope you'll be lucky enough to survive the trek back to civilization to talk about it!

THE END

To follow another path, turn to page 11.
To learn more about the Lost Dutchman's Gold Mine, turn to page 103.

"We need water, Marta," you groan. "Like, right now."

The two of you head over to a few cacti. Marta doesn't look so sure, but you shrug it off.

"Here goes nothin'," you say.

You take out your knife and cut a hole in the base of a cactus, being careful not to poke yourself on its spines. Almost instantly, a stream of cloudy water starts to pour out. You cup your hands to catch some of the liquid and drink it. The cactus juice is bitter and tastes terrible.

Marta drinks some of the water too and gags. Although it tastes awful, you both drink until the cactus is empty. But a few minutes later, you can feel your stomach wrench.

"Maybe this is the wrong kind of cactus," you groan, holding your gut.

People sometimes think they can drink cactus water to survive in the desert. But cactuses are very acidic and unsafe for people to eat or drink.

Both of you bend over and vomit up all of the cactus water. You feel even worse than before. Being sick in the middle of the desert isn't good. As you lie down in the sand, you can almost hear the vultures above you getting ready for a big meal.

THE END

To follow another path, turn to page 11.
To learn more about the Lost Dutchman's Gold Mine, turn to page 103.

The Superstition Mountain Museum
includes buildings once used for making
old western movies.

CHAPTER 4

THIS BELONGS IN A MUSEUM!

"It's probably best to start with the clues that have already been found," you say after your plane lands. "That means checking out the Superstition Mountain Museum."

"Good idea," Marta replies. "I was kind of hoping you'd say that. Those stone maps that people have been trying to figure out seem like a great place to start."

You're eager to start your search for both the mine and your lost brother, James. You're pretty sure James has already studied the stones or even memorized what is on them. So following in his footsteps seems like the best option.

Turn the page.

As you arrive at the museum, you scan the Sonoran Desert and the mountains nearby. The mountains look foreboding, and you sweat just looking at the desert. But the good news is the museum is close to both areas. That will make the search a little easier.

You climb out of the car, and the Arizona sun reminds you again just how hot it is here. Marta shades her eyes and looks out at the mountains and desert. She's already looking for James. You're glad she decided to join you.

Inside the air-conditioned museum you see exhibits about animals in the area. Many more creatures live out in the desert than you expected. Not many of them look friendly. You can't help but wonder if you might run into some of these creatures when you're out exploring later.

The Arizona desert is home to several poisonous animals such as scorpions and rattlesnakes.

Marta points to a section that displays pottery made by Indigenous people along with some of the minerals found in the mountains. Learning about the area's geology might be a good idea. You're both here to see the Peralta Stone maps, but looking at some of the other exhibits first might be useful.

To look at the wildlife exhibits, turn to page 76.

To study the minerals, turn to page 78.

"Maybe I'm being overly cautious," you say. "But knowing what sort of animals are out there in the desert and mountains might be helpful."

"You're probably right," Marta says, eyeing a stuffed coyote on a fake rock.

You've never been to the desert before, so you're not familiar with what sort of creatures live in the hot, sandy, and rocky terrain. You and Marta study the exhibit. In a display case you see a mean-looking mountain lion. In addition, there are eagles, hawks, and a few types of vultures.

"If we see these guys circling in the air, it means they're looking for food," Marta says, pointing at the vulture.

That's news to you. You always thought that circling vultures meant they found something dead on the ground. In the movies it usually means someone didn't survive in the desert.

Across the room, you find a display of the different snakes found in the desert and mountains. One of them catches your eye. It's the Sonoran coral snake. It has red, white, and black bands of color along its body. You read further and see that its venom is like a cobra's. You shudder. Snakes are *not* your favorite animal.

You've read that a lot of people have gone missing while searching for the mine. But you wonder if some of them were attacked by wild animals out in the hot Sonoran Desert. You take in as much as you can before it's time to look at the Peralta Stones.

Turn to page 80.

"I think we should look at some of the rocks and minerals in the area," you suggest. "It might help us figure out where this lost gold mine actually is."

"You want to look at rocks?" Marta asks. "With James lost somewhere out there?"

"It won't take too long," you promise.

You know James might be out in the desert somewhere. He could be lost or hurt. The clock is ticking. But since you're not familiar with the Sonoran Desert or the Superstition Mountains, it doesn't hurt to learn a little about the terrain.

You and Marta look at the glass cases that display the different types of rocks and minerals in the nearby mountains and desert. You learn that much of the Superstition Mountains are a result of volcanic activity. Some of the large rock formations were welded together by hot lava.

Some of the other rocks are beautifully shiny and look like gold. But you quickly learn that they're not gold at all.

"Fool's gold," Marta says. "A lot of miners in the past believed they found gold. But they later discovered that the gold was really iron pyrite."

"What a bummer," you say, shaking your head. "Imagine thinking you were rich beyond your wildest dreams, only to find out that it's almost worthless."

Turn the page.

Iron pyrite looks very similar to real gold.

"Let's go check out the Peralta Stones," you suggest. "That lost mine and James aren't going to find themselves!"

You and Marta head over to where the Peralta Stones are displayed. They are four rectangular stones with carvings on them.

Two stones have writing etched into their surfaces. One of these has a carving of a horse. Another stone has a heart that looks like it can be removed and a carving of a knife. The fourth stone seems to have a character holding a cross or a hammer and some numbers etched into it.

Studying them further, you can see what looks like little mountains and a path with dots on them. Are those trail markers? Scrawled on the stone heart are several Spanish words.

"That one says 'Falling golden water'," Marta says. "The cross says 'Cave of Hat Mountain'."

You take a picture of the stones and carvings. A few locations on the map look promising. One squiggly line on the stones leads to a dot in the middle of the heart. Another is what looks like a cave near a hat-shaped mountain.

"What's next?" Marta asks.

To look for the "Hat Mountain" cave, turn to page 82.

To look for the center of the heart, turn to page 84.

Some people believe the mysterious Peralta Stones hold the secret to the Lost Dutchman's Mine. Many others think the stones are fake.

"I think we should look for this Hat Mountain," you say. "The little wizard guy is holding a cross, and it says Hat Mountain. Maybe he's pointing to the location?"

Marta smiles. "And just like magic, that lost gold mine will appear," she teases.

"Very funny," you say, chuckling.

You and Marta head toward the state park near the mountains and find a spot to park the car. As you climb out, you put on a hat to shield yourself from the sun. As you do, Marta stops you.

"Wait a second," she says, grabbing your hat. "Look at this!"

She holds the hat out in front of her. The hat almost perfectly covers a boxy portion of the mountains that looks like . . . a hat.

"Hat mountain?" Marta offers with a shrug.

"Works for me," you say.

It's the best lead you've gotten so far, so it's worth a shot. You study the landscape and marvel at how much desert there is out there. The mountains don't look much friendlier. Despite the heat, you shiver a bit as you think of all the people who have disappeared in the area. You just hope you and Marta won't be joining them.

You look through the park and see a trail that leads toward the hat-shaped mountain. But somehow it seems too easy. You wonder if you'll have better luck striking off on your own.

To follow the trail to Hat Mountain, turn to page 86.

To go off the trail and see what you can find, turn to page 88.

"That removable heart piece seems to be important," you say, staring at the heart.

You study the markings closely. It appears that the start of the trail is at the base of the mountain and ends with an *X* at the center of the stone heart. Could the end of the trail be the location of the Lost Dutchman's Gold Mine? You hope so.

You and Marta head toward the mountain. As she drives, you study the photos you took of the stone heart. You compare its markings to the landmarks you see along the mountains' ridgeline. You also notice small circles among the markings. Could those be caves or mine shafts?

When you reach the base of the mountain, you look for anything that might resemble a trail. You notice a path winding upward through some brush and cacti to the left. It seems to snake around some smaller boulders and up near a taller rock formation.

The Siphon Draw trail at Lost Dutchman State Park, Arizona

If the map is to be trusted, it seems the trail might lead to a cave where there's a carving of a dagger. But then Marta points toward a barely visible path to the right near a large cluster of rocks.

To follow the winding trail, turn to page 90.
To go on the faded path, turn to page 92.

Based on what you saw at the museum, there are lots of wild animals out in the Sonoran Desert. It would be foolish to stray too far off the trail.

You follow a bunch of other people who are there to hike. It's hot out and you're sweating—a lot. You're just glad you brought plenty of water to drink. You scan the side of the mountain for any sign of a cave.

Marta asks other hikers if they know where the caves are in Hat Mountain. They look confused, and none of them seem familiar with the name. You realize Hat Mountain might not be called that anymore.

You spend hours looking for the cave. When you get higher up, you're able to see all sorts of other mountains in the area. There are literally a million places to look for James.

The rugged Superstition Mountains cover nearly 250 square miles (650 square kilometers) of land.

"Now I understand how people disappear out in the Superstition Mountains," you say. "It'll take forever to explore all of this."

You spend a week looking for your brother and the mine. Sadly, you never find either.

THE END

To follow another path, turn to page 11.
To learn more about the Lost Dutchman's Gold Mine, turn to page 103.

"If James is lost, he won't be hanging out on some hiking trail," you say. "Knowing my brother, he probably ventured off in some unexplored area."

"You're right," Marta agrees. "That sounds like him."

The two of you decide to go off the trail to explore the desert and head toward the mountain. It's hot, and you feel dizzy after a few hours of hiking through the rough terrain. There's little shade, and the sun is beating down on you. You feel like you might melt where you stand.

As you get closer to the mountain, you scan everywhere looking for any sign of a cave or even some shade. But there doesn't seem to be anything of the sort. After a while, you resort to shouting for James.

"JAAAAAMES!"

But you only hear echoes off in the distance.

"If James is out here, he had to have heard that," Marta says. "I think most of Arizona heard you."

As the sun starts to set, you think it would be smart to quit for the day. You turn to head back, but you don't see your vehicle or the parking lot. You check your phone, but see that you have no signal out here.

You and Marta start walking in what you think is the right direction. As the sky grows darker, you hear a low growl.

"Run!" Marta cries out. You turn to see a mountain lion coming your way. You don't know if mountain lion attacks are fatal, but you're about to find out!

THE END

To follow another path, turn to page 11.
To learn more about the Lost Dutchman's Gold Mine, turn to page 103.

"Let's go up there," you say, pointing to the cluster of brush and cacti.

"Might as well," Marta says with a shrug. "That so-called map on the Peralta Stones isn't much help."

You begin to follow the winding trail along the left side. The way is tricky to navigate, and sweating from the extreme heat doesn't make things easier. But you and Marta help each other climb up where you can.

Any time you hear a noise in the brush, you're almost sure it's a snake coming to take a bite out of you. Finally, after what feels like hours, you find yourself near one of the rocky spires. You look at the photo of the stone maps again.

"Do you think the knife on the map is a symbol for a taller rock formation?" you ask, showing Marta the photo.

"I'm not sure," she says. "The other mountains were carved as squiggly lines. Why would that one be different?"

You continue walking. As you go along, you wipe your sweaty face with your shirt. Just then, you step onto a thatched mat hidden by rocks and sand. You fall into a deep pitfall trap. Sharp blades pierce your side as you look up and see Marta's shocked face. You glance around to see the whole pit full of blades and spikes.

Oh, so that's what the knife meant, you think as you fade away.

THE END

To follow another path, turn to page 11.
To learn more about the Lost Dutchman's Gold Mine, turn to page 103.

"It doesn't look like anyone has gone that way," Marta explains, still pointing at the almost-hidden path she found.

"You might be on to something," you tell Marta. "Let's check it out."

The path Marta found seems to make the most sense. When you look at the map again, you can almost line up the mountains etchings on the Peralta Stones with the formations in front of you.

You press on, looking for landmarks that might be represented on the stones.

At one point, you pass through a small valley that looks similar to an area on the map. You feel good about the path you've taken. You don't want to get too excited, but you seem to be on the right path! You wonder if James made it this far in his search for the Lost Dutchman's mine.

As you approach where you think the *X* on the stones is, you point it out to Marta.

"Looks like we're getting close," she says. "*X* marks the spot. Isn't that what treasure hunters say?"

As you look up, you notice a tangle of dead shrubs propped up against a rock wall. It's sort of hidden behind a cluster of rocks. When you get close, you notice there are boards behind the shrubs, as if sealing something up. The map seems to show that you should keep going. But could this be the mine?

To press on to the heart of the mountain, turn to page 94.

To see what's behind the boards, turn to page 96.

"It seems unlikely that nobody would find the mine here," you say.

"Yes," Marta agrees. "This location would be too easy."

There's no way that the Lost Dutchman's mine is behind the boards. But just in case, you call out your brother's name into the boarded-up cave. There's no answer. You can only hope that James didn't end up in there and got himself hurt.

After you and Marta drink a little water, you start to move up the mountain again. It is slow going, but the two of you manage to get further up. It's hot and dusty work. As you stop to rest, you hear something quietly scraping along the rocks. Marta's eyes are wide with fear.

"Is that an animal?" Marta whispers. She looks frozen in place as if she's afraid to move. You freeze too, looking for any sign of trouble.

You quickly think about some of the wild animals you saw displayed in the museum. Now you're wishing you would've paid closer attention. You're not sure if it's an animal but wonder if moving away quickly would be the safe decision.

To get out of there, turn to page 98.

To see what's making the noise, turn to page 100.

Mountain lions are stealthy hunters in Arizona's mountains.

You decide that you have to see what's behind those boards.

"If this is the lost mine, I'm surprised nobody's found it," you say.

"Maybe no one noticed the boards hidden behind the rocks," Marta adds.

The two of you pull some of the boards free until there's a big enough space to squeeze through. You climb through and click on your flashlights to take a look around.

You don't see any footprints or other signs. It seems nobody has been in here for a long time. You move forward, carefully walking past old crates, mining equipment, and support beams.

Then your flashlight shines on something sparkling on the ground. It looks like a gold nugget! You can hardly contain your excitement. Did you just find the Lost Dutchman's mine?

"What did you find?" Marta asks.

"Gold!" you reply back. "A gold nugget, Marta!"

You continue forward and find a large mined-out space in the mountain. Everywhere you look, you can see gold.

"I can't believe it!" you shout. "This is it!"

Marta shrieks in excitement, and the two of you can't believe your luck. A few days later, you bring in a geologist to examine the mine.

"I'm sorry to tell you this," the geologist says, shaking her head, "but you found a mine full of fool's gold."

Not only did you not find the Lost Dutchman's mine, but you didn't find James either.

THE END
To follow another path, turn to page 11.
To learn more about the Lost Dutchman's Gold Mine, turn to page 103.

"Let's get out of here," you suggest. "I love animals, but not wild ones."

It's better to be safe than sorry, so you move away as quickly as you can. Further up the mountain you notice a rusted metal ring fixed into the rock face. When you look up, there's a ledge above you.

You've never been a rock climber, but you manage to pull yourself up onto the ledge. After helping Marta up, you find yourself standing in front of the opening to a very well-hidden mine shaft.

"You think this is it?" Marta asks.

You shrug. "There's only one way to find out," you reply.

The two of you walk into the shaft and notice several antique tools and other equipment. You call out for James, but there's no response.

After searching the entire mine, you don't find anything. As you turn to leave, Marta stops and picks up something shiny. It's small but looks promising. You remember that real gold is soft. You press the edge of your knife to the surface, and it leaves a mark.

"This might've been the lost mine," you say. "But it seems it was found a long time ago."

You bend over to pick up a worn leather helmet. Branded into the leather are the initials J.W. Did this belong to Jacob Waltz?

It seems you may have found the Lost Dutchman's mine. Unfortunately, there's no gold left here to claim.

THE END

To follow another path, turn to page 11.
To learn more about the Lost Dutchman's Gold Mine, turn to page 103.

"I'm not sure an animal is making that noise," you say, listening carefully.

You carefully step around the brush and rocks blocking your view, prepared for the worst.

As you move around the obstacles, you can hear a wheezing noise. There on the ground is your brother, James! He looks terrible, as if he hasn't eaten in days. He's clutching his leg and when he sees you, he just shakes his head.

"It's me, James," you say. "Are you okay?"

Your brother seems out of it, almost like he doesn't believe it's you.

"I . . . I didn't find it," James rasps. He shakes his head.

"Don't worry about that," you say. "We're just glad we found you. Everyone has been worried sick!"

You give him some water, and he drinks it slowly, coughing a bit as he swallows. Marta looks at his leg.

"I think his leg is broken," she says. "We need to get him out of here and to a hospital."

The two of you work together to help James down off the mountain. You may not have found the Lost Dutchman's mine, but at least you found your lost brother. Well done!

THE END

To follow another path, turn to page 11.
To learn more about the Lost Dutchman's Gold Mine, turn to page 103.

CHAPTER 5

THE TREASURE IS MINE! ALL MINE!

What was the Lost Dutchman's Gold Mine? Did it actually exist? It all depends on whether the stories about its history are true or not.

The Superstition Mountains have always been a mysterious place. There are caves and signs that people once lived there, though no one is sure who the people were. In the 1800s, the Apache people who occupied the area turned the mountains into their stronghold.

In the 1840s, the Peralta family from northern Mexico began mining for gold in the Superstition Mountains. They transported it back to Mexico by horse and wagon.

The Peraltas' last "gold run" happened in 1848. That caravan was attacked by the Apache, and nearly all of the Peraltas were killed. Only two members of the Peralta family survived the attack.

Word spread about the Peraltas' fortune and their demise. Eager to find their mine, many people made maps and claimed to know where it was. During this time, several people who searched the area disappeared or died from unexplained accidents. These events added to the legend of the Superstition Mountains and the lost mine.

In the 1870s, a man named Jacob Waltz claimed a member of the Peralta family shared the mine's location with him. People in town even noticed him using gold nuggets to pay for things.

It was believed Waltz and his partner, Jacob Weiser, worked the mine and hid a large stash of gold somewhere in the Superstition Mountains.

Weiser was later killed by the Apache. However, some people believe that Waltz murdered his partner to keep the fortune for himself.

About 20 years later, Waltz's health was failing. His neighbor, Julia Thomas, took care of him. Julia claimed that Waltz told her where the mine was before he died. She and a crew looked for the mine but couldn't find it. Thousands of other treasure seekers have tried and failed as well. Many have died or disappeared while searching, which has kept the mountains' spooky reputation alive and well.

Did the Lost Dutchman's Gold Mine even exist? And if so, is it still out there? To this day, treasure hunters are still searching for the lost mine and its hidden gold.

Other Lost Treasures Around the World

THE HONJO MASAMUNE

This historic sword was made by Japanese blacksmith Goro Nyudo Masamune. He was considered the best sword maker in history. The sword was named after samurai Honjo Shigenaga, who survived an attack from the blade in the 16th century. He took the fabled sword as a souvenir of his near-death experience. Sometime after World War II, the sword was lost and never seen again.

THE CROWN JEWELS OF IRELAND

These valuable jewels were stolen from Dublin Castle in 1907. The jewels were used to create a diamond brooch. The treasure is made up of 394 stones from Queen Charlotte's jewelry along with an Order of the Oath badge. The jewels were displayed in the castle's library until they disappeared and were never recovered.

ROMANOV EASTER EGGS

In 1885, Russia's royal Romanov family had master goldsmith Peter Carl Fabergé design unique egg-shaped treasures. They were covered in gold and jewels. Inside each egg was an additional valuable item. There were 50 eggs in all, but eight of them were lost over time.

TOMB OF GENGHIS KHAN

When the Mongolian warrior leader Genghis Khan died, his body was brought to the Burkhan Khaldun Mountains in Mongolia. He wanted to be buried with some of his treasures in an unmarked grave where no one could find him. Some legends say the soldiers who brought him there were killed to keep the location a secret. Hundreds of year later, no one knows where Genghis Khan is buried.

THE AMBER ROOM

In the 1700s, Prussia gave the Amber Room to Russia as a gift of peace and friendship. It was located in St. Petersburg, Russia. The walls were made of large panels of amber covered with gold and precious jewels. Today the room would be worth about $200 million. But during World War II (1939–1945) German troops invaded Russia and stole the Amber Room. The priceless treasure has been missing ever since.

OTHER PATHS TO EXPLORE

>>> In your search for James and the Lost Dutchman's Gold Mine, you explored some pretty rough terrain. What would you bring to make the quest easier to handle? Are there things you couldn't live without? Are there different places you might search for the mine instead?

>>> The Superstition Mountains are known for being a dangerous place. People have been killed, lost, or severely injured in their search for riches. Do you believe it's as dangerous as everyone thinks? Is it possible that some of the stories are just tall tales?

>>> Nobody has yet found the Lost Dutchman's mine or any gold. There are plenty of caves and mine shafts in the mountains. Do you think the mine may have already been found? What do you think happened to Jacob Waltz's gold?

BIBLIOGRAPHY

"America Unearthed: Lost Dutchman Gold Mine Discovered in Arizona," History, Youtube.com, January 3, 2021, https://www.youtube.com/watch?v=oRSu_NwpwhM.

"Clay Worst Dutchman Lecture 2006," Youtube.com, November 28, 2015, https://www.youtube.com/watch?v=40eH6xQ-U9M.

"Has the Lost Dutchman Mine Been Found?" by Bob Willis, True West: History of the American Frontier, April 1, 2005, https://truewestmagazine.com/article/has-the-lost-dutchman-mine-been-found/.

"Legend of the Lost Dutchman," Arizona State Parks, https://azstateparks.com/lost-dutchman/explore/the-dutchman.

"The Lost Dutchman Mine, Arizona," by Kathy Weiser, Legends of America, November 2019, https://www.legendsofamerica.com/az-lostdutchman/.

"Peralta Stones Map and the Stone Crosses," by Robert L. and Lynda R. Kesselring, Desert USA, https://www.desertusa.com/lost-dutchman/peralta-stones2/peralta-gold2.html.

"Where is the Lost Dutchman Mine?" by William Pitts, 12 News Arizona, May 13, 2022, https://www.12news.com/article/news/local/arizona/where-is-the-lost-dutchman-mine-in-arizona/75-f0a88f0e-9060-4b7c-9aa4-07cbdf0300c3.

GLOSSARY

camouflage (KA-muh-flahzh)—coloring or covering that makes animals, people, or objects look like their surroundings

crevasse (krih-VASS)—a deep, wide crack in a glacier or the earth

foliage (FOH-lee-ij)—the leaves of a plant

geology (jee-AH-luh-jee)—the study of minerals, rocks, and soil

hydrated (HYE-dray-tuhd)—to have a healthy balance of fluids in the body

Indigenous (in-DIH-juh-nuhs)—native to a place

machete (muh-SHEH-tee)—a long, heavy knife with a broad blade used to cut underbrush or as a weapon

mirage (muh-RAZH)—something that appears to be there but is not, such as a body of water

ominous (AH-muh-nuhs)—a sign of possible future harmful events

stalagmite (stuh-LAG-mahyt)—a rocky formation that stands on the floor of a cave and is created by drips of water from above

superstition (soo-puhr-STIH-shuhn)—a belief or irrational fear that a particular place or thing has dangerous supernatural qualities

READ MORE

Hyde, Natalie. *Gold Rushes*. New York: Crabtree Publishing, 2018.

Rusick, Jessica. *Joining the California Gold Rush: A This or That Debate*. North Mankato, MN: Capstone Press, 2020.

Troupe, Thomas Kingsley. *Can You Spot Blackbeard's Treasure?: An Interactive Treasure Adventure*. North Mankato, MN: Capstone Press, 2023.

INTERNET SITES

Legend of the Lost Dutchman
azstateparks.com/lost-dutchman/explore/the-dutchman

The Lost Dutchman Gold Mine
jamesmdeem.com/stories.treasure.dutchman.html

Lost Dutchman Mine
legendsofamerica.com/az-lostdutchman/

Lost Dutchman State Park Facts for Kids
kids.kiddle.co/Lost_Dutchman_State_Park

ABOUT THE AUTHOR

Thomas Kingsley Troupe is the author of more than 200 books for young readers. He's written books about everything from third grade werewolves to ballerinas to talking spaceships. He's even written a book about dirt. Thomas wrote his first book when he was in second grade and has been making up stories ever since. When he's not behind the keyboard, he enjoys reading, playing video games, and hunting ghosts with the Twin Cities Paranormal Society. Otherwise, he's probably taking a nap or something. Thomas lives in Woodbury, Minnesota, with his two sons.